Community Service Opportunities for High School Students:

200+ Ideas for Service, Eagle Awards, Gold Awards, and Capstones

Rachel A. Winston, Ph.D.

www.collegelizard.com

rwinston@uchicago.edu

Service is a selfless commitment to your community.

Discover opportunities for you to make the world a better place now and in the future!

Why Trust Me?

In my four decades as a college counselor and professor have walked thousands of students through the chaos and confusion of college admissions, from first-gen applicants, unsure where to start, to high-achievers dreaming of top-tier universities.

As a professor, college advisor, and admissions coach with degrees from UCLA, Harvard, UChicago, Claremont Graduate University, Pepperdine, GWU, CSUF, CSUDH, Syracuse, Gallaudet, and more, I have helped students craft compelling applications and essays that go beyond grades and statistics.

I have also written and published 40+ books on college admission available on Amazon, including my recent best-selling 350-page book for high school students, "Medical School Bound".

Whether it is cracking the code on admissions or navigating waitlists, I have seen what works and created this guide to give you that exact edge.

ISBNs - paperback 978-1-958558-54-6, E-book 978-1-958558-55-3

LCCN: 2025915930

We work with academic leaders who transform the educational landscape to publish relevant content and advise students of their educational and professional options, with the aim of developing 21st-century learners and leaders. We also work with students to publish their books and present widely diverse ideas to the college/graduate school-bound community. With headquarters in Irvine, California, Lizard Publishing works virtually with authors to edit, publish, and distribute both hard copy and digital books.

Th is book was published in the U.S.A. Lizard Publishing is a premium quality provider of educational reference, career guidance, and motivational publications/merchandise for global learners, educators, and stakeholders in education.

Book formatting by Obinna Chinemerem Ozuo

Book website: www.collegelizard.com

About the Author

Dr. Rachel A. Winston is a tireless student advocate. She has served the educational community as a university professor, college advisor, statistician, researcher, author, cryptanalyst, motivational speaker, publishing executive, and lifelong student. As one of the leading experts in college counseling and an award-winning faculty member, Dr. Winston has spent her lifetime learning, teaching, mentoring, and coaching students. Her counseling practice centers around college admissions, college essays, portfolios, and intellectual conversations about life and career pursuits.

She started college at thirteen and graduated from college programs in such widely ranging disciplines as chemistry, mathematics, computers, liberal arts, international relations, negotiation, conflict resolution, peacebuilding, business administration, higher education leadership, interpreting, college counseling, and publishing. Throughout her education, she attended and graduated from Harvard, University of Chicago, University of Texas, GWU, UCLA, Syracuse, CSUF, CSUDH, Pepperdine, Claremont Graduate University, and Gallaudet University.

Her position working in Washington, D.C. on Capitol Hill and with the White House in the 1980s took her to approximately a hundred universities training campaign managers at colleges from Colorado to California, thoroughly dotting the western states. Later, she led college tours with students and their families on road trips throughout the United States. She has taught or counseled thousands of students over her career and speaks at conferences and academic programs throughout the world.

As a professor and avid writer for numerous publications, she won the 2012 McFarland Literary Achievement Award, Bletchley Park Cryptanalyst Award, and numerous other awards, including Faculty Member of the Year, Leadership Tomorrow Leader of the Year, and college service and leadership awards. While studying Human Capital at Claremont Graduate University, she was a scholarship recipient at the Drucker School of Management. She was also elected to the statewide Board of Governors for the Faculty Association for California Community Colleges, where she served on their executive committee.

She also served as a faculty member for the UCLA College Counselor Certificate Program and the Director of Mathematics at Brandman University. She taught at Embry Riddle Aeronautical University, Chapman University, Cal State Fullerton, and a handful of California Community Colleges, including Cerro Coso College where she represented the entire faculty as the Academic Senate President and retired in 2016. Over her career, she taught mathematics on television, in small and large lecture halls, online, and via live interactive satellite and telecourses.

.

Table of Contents

Chapter 1:
National & International Awards

1. President's Volunteer Service Award

By starting now and accumulating hours, you can earn one of the following Presidential awards.

Participating in the President's Volunteer Service Award is a powerful testament to the transformative potential of service. The honor represents the character of those who give of themselves to improve the lives of others. It recognizes hours spent by individuals whose hearts are opened, while lifting up their communities. Each winner is acknowledged for their sense of unity forged through action. At its core, the Presidential Volunteer Service Award affirms that even in a fast-paced, digital world, compassion and civic engagement still matter.

Recipients of the Presidential Volunteer Service Award build bridges between generations and connect people with humanitarian causes. They tutor children, care for the elderly, deliver meals, clean parks, serve veterans, raise awareness, and extend empathy where it is most needed. These acts of kindness, whether they are visible or unseen, create ripples of good that outlast the moment. For students, this award fosters a habit of service that extends beyond school requirements and résumés. It encourages reflection, responsibility, and the development of a moral compass calibrated toward justice, dignity, and inclusion.

Presidential Volunteer Service Award

Hours Required to Earn Awards in Each Age Group				
Age Group	**Bronze**	**Silver**	**Gold**	**Lifetime Achievement Award**
Kids (5-10 years old)	26-49 hours	50-74 hours	75+ hours	4,000+ hours
Teens (11-15)	50-74 hours	75-99 hours	100+ hours	4,000+ hours
Young Adults (16-25)	100--174 hours	175-249 hours	250+ hours	4,000+ hours
Adults (26+)	100-249 hours	250-499 hours	500+ hours	4,000+ hours

2. The Congressional Award

- **Who is eligible?** Youth aged 13½ to under 24. (There is no GPA requirement.)
- **Requirements:** Complete hours in four areas:
  - Voluntary Public Service
  - Physical Fitness
  - Personal Development
  - Expedition/Exploration
- **Award Levels:**
  - *Bronze/Silver/Gold Certificates*: 60–180+ hours
  - *Medals*: 200–800+ hours plus multi-month commitment

3. Prudential Spirit of Community Awards *(Emerging Visionaries)*

- **Who is eligible?** U.S. resident, students in grades 5–12
- **Requirements:**
  - Volunteer service at least partly in the prior 12 months.
  - Application; certification by school principal or approved organization
- **Recognition Levels:**
  - Local Honorees: Certificates
  - State Honorees: $1,000 scholarship, silver medallion, trip to DC
  - National Honorees: $5,000 scholarship, gold medallion, grants

4. Jefferson Awards (Multiplying Good)

- **Eligibility:** Varies; teen categories exist for middle/high school students

- **Nomination:** Local/city level for their community or public service
- **Criteria:** Sustained service, impact, and leadership
- **Prizes:** Local, state, and national

5. Gloria Barron Prize for Young Heroes

- **Eligibility:** 8–18 years old
- **Criteria:** Significant, sustained effort in service/environmental stewardship
- **Process:** Nomination-based; application and impact statements
- **Winners:** 25 annually receive a citation and have their work publicized

6. The Diana Award (International Award)

- **Age range:** 9–25 years
- **Criteria:** Global, including U.S. students making a positive impact
- **Process:** Nomination/application; leadership, community benefit, commitment
- **Awards** Physical award, mentorship, networking, and support

7. Duke of Edinburgh's (International Award)

- **Eligibility:** 14–24, including in the U.S.
- Program Areas:
  - Voluntary Service
  - Skill-Building
  - Physical Recreation
  - Adventurous Journ
- **Awards:** Bronze, Silver, Gold
- **Requires** Supervisor/advisor (school/youth organizations)

8. Ashoka Young Changemakers (International Award)

- **Age range:** Under 20.
- **Eligibility:** Youth leading social impact projects.
- **Application:** Project description, impact evidence, social-change vision.
- **Award:** Mentorship, global community belonging, and promotion.

Final Thoughts

In an era when individual achievement often takes center stage, community service highlights the importance of collective action and selflessness. Helping others offers a counter-narrative to a world that prizes prestige and performance by spotlighting those who lead with humility and serve without expectation. These awards remind us that some of the most important work is done without recognition in shelters, hospitals, classrooms, and neighborhoods.

Engaging in service at a young age is profound. Refocusing on the needs of others equips students with empathy, resilience, and perspective. It fosters cultural awareness and a lifelong commitment to the common good. Those who earn these awards are often transformed by their experiences. They discover a cause important to them or a career that aligns with their values.

Ultimately, serving community members and the planet we live on affirms that every person, regardless of their age or background, has the power to be a catalyst for change. It celebrates the radical but straightforward truth that service is not an obligation, but a passion and commitment to making this world a better place. Join a legacy of hope for our shared humanity.

Chapter 2:
Community & National Volunteer Organizations

Community and national service organizations offer middle and high school students transformative experiences that go far beyond volunteer hours. These organizations cultivate empathy, leadership, and civic responsibility at a pivotal stage in personal development. Whether students organize food drives with Key Club, mentor peers through Best Buddies, assemble care packages with National Charity League, or build homes with Habitat for Humanity, they are exposed to real-world challenges and the power of collaborative solutions.

These organizations foster long-term character formation. They teach discipline, teamwork, and time management while connecting students to causes larger than themselves. Students learn that their voices matter and that advocacy, compassion, and hands-on effort can change lives. They gain insight into social justice, inequality, and the realities of underserved populations.

These programs also offer a safe and empowering space for students to step into leadership roles, build confidence, and forge lasting friendships. In an increasingly competitive world, service allows young people to find purpose. From the structure of Lion's Heart and Boys Team Charity to the global outreach of Operation Smile, these groups open doors to personal growth, scholarship opportunities, and intergenerational impact.

Collectively, they shape a generation not just to succeed, but to serve, creating ripple effects across families, schools, and communities. The enduring impact of these organizations is invaluable to our communities.

American Red Cross Youth Services

Assistance League

Best Buddies International

Big Brothers Big Sisters of America

Boy Scouts of America

Boys Team Charity

BuildOn

California Scholarship Federation

Catholic Charities USA Youth Programs

DoSomething.org

Feeding America Youth Engagement

Girl Scouts of the USA

Girls Team Charity

Habitat for Humanity Youth Programs

HandsOn Connect / Points of Light Youth Network

Hugh O'Brian Youth Leadership

Key Club International

Lions Clubs International's Leo Clubs

Lion's Heart Teen Volunteers

Meals on Wheels Volunteer Programs

National Charity League

National Honor Society

National Junior Honor Society

National League of Young Men

Operation Smile Student Programs

Ronald McDonald House Youth Volunteers

Special Olympics Youth Volunteer Program

The Trevor Project – Youth Ambassador Program

United Way Youth Engagement

Young Men's Service League

Chapter 3:
Translating Passion into Action
Ideas for Showing Passion for College Applications

American Cancer Society

Project: Relay For Life – Youth or School Team
Start or join a student-led team to participate in a local Relay For Life event, which raises funds for cancer research, patient support, and awareness campaigns. Students organize team fundraising efforts (e.g., bake sales, car washes, online campaigns) and participate in the community walk event.

Goal: Raise cancer awareness and funds to support research, transportation for patients, and services like Hope Lodge. Build teamwork, leadership, and advocacy skills while making a meaningful difference in the lives of those affected by cancer.

College Application: Emphasize the creation of a partnership with the American Cancer Society through Relay For Life. Explain how you led a youth fundraising team, organized awareness events at school, and spoke at a community gathering honoring cancer survivors. Discuss how much money you raised and what the experience meant to you in terms of relationships, leaderships, insights, and challenges you had to overcome.

American Heart Association

Project: Youth Advocacy and Awareness Campaign
Start or join a school-based initiative in partnership with the American Heart Association to educate peers about heart attack prevention, treatment disparities, early detection, and ongoing research. With one in every five deaths in the U.S. per year (nearly 700,000 deaths yearly), heart disease is the biggest killer of Americans. Organize awareness days, educational presentations, poster campaigns, and social media outreach to engage your school community.

Goal: Increase awareness and understanding of heart disease among youth. Promote healthy lifestyle choices, early screening knowledge, and equity in healthcare access. Advocate for research funding and public policies that support patients and survivors. Encourage informed conversations around heart attacks and dispel myths through evidence-based information.

College Application: Discuss your role in the student-led heart disease awareness campaign with the American Heart Association, Explain what you accomplished and what it meant to you to lead peer education sessions focused on prevention, early detection, and research advancements. Describe what it took to produce informational displays during National CPR & AED Awareness Week and any organizations or professionals you contacted. If you had Q&A panels, collaborations, or initiatives, what did you do or learn?

Backpacks for Education

Project: Collect backpacks and supplies for underserved schools; hold a reflection session before delivery.

Goal: Organize your efforts through your school, youth leadership organization, or teen board.

College Application Suggestion: Highlight logistics, compassion, and broad community impact.

"Blessing Bags" for the Homeless

Project: Assemble and distribute care packages with toiletries, snacks, socks, and handwritten notes.

Goal: Set up a drive through your congregation of any religious denomination.

College Application Suggestion: Highlight empathy, initiative, and collaboration with local shelters.

Eco-Awareness Day: "The Earth is Our Sacred Ground"

Project: Create a composting site, native plant garden, or recycling initiative as an expression of care for nature and the Earth's creation.

Goal: Set up this event at a park, forest, beach, or eco-area.

College Application Suggestion: Link sustainability with stewardship for the land.

Holiday Service Projects - Christmas, Channukah, Diwali, Easter, Eid, Halloween, Ramadan, Passover, Thanksgiving

Project: Organize a toy, book, or winter clothing drive around major holidays.

Goal: In collaboration with a faith-based youth committee.

College Application Suggestion: Emphasize seasonal outreach and mobilizing peers.

Interfaith Service Day

Project: Organize a service day where youth from different faiths collaborate on a shared project (e.g., park clean-up, community mural, food drive).

Goal: Promote unity, peace, and dialogue.

College Application Suggestion: Emphasize leadership, cross-cultural communication, and civic responsibility.

"Peace Wall" or "Social Justice Art Wall"

Project: Lead a youth art project that expresses values shared across cultures, emphasizing hope, compassion, and justice.

Goal: Display it in your worship space or local community center.

College Application Suggestion: Reflect on creative leadership and bridge-building.

"Quotes for Inspiration" Series

Project: Create short videos or graphics with weekly inspirational quotes, reflections, prayers, or verses shared via your group's social media sites.

Goal: Post on Instagram, YouTube, and TikTok for impact and empowerment.

College Application Suggestion: Blend technology and outreach for a unique portfolio piece.

Refugee Welcome Day

Project: Volunteer through a leadership or service group to tutor children or teens in English, math, or reading.

Goal: Provide outreach programs to those who are new to America with translation services and community-organized support.

College Application Suggestion: Note your sense of cultural humility and educational impact.

"Sacred Soup Sunday"

Project: Cook and serve a meal weekly or monthly for those in need. This could be for the elderly, disenfranchised, refugees, houseless, or disabled veterans.

Goal: You can set this up at your school, community center, partner organization or place of worship.

College Application Suggestion: Showcase consistency, planning skills, and personal growth.

Storytelling Night: "Empowerment in Action"

Project: Host an evening where youth share stories of how they inspire and translate their vision into service.

Goal: Partner with centers to create a speaker panel or take turns speaking among your group.

College Application Suggestion: Mention public speaking, event planning, and empathy.

Chapter 4:
Animals, Marine Life, Wildlife

Assisting animals, whether domestic pets, marine life, or wildlife, is a powerful and compassionate act of service that nurtures empathy, responsibility, and global awareness. Precious pets require more than just food and shelter; they need enrichment, play, love, and medical attention to thrive. By volunteering at a shelter, fostering cats or dogs, assisting at adoption events, or supporting a veterinary clinic, students provide essential care to creatures who often cannot advocate for themselves. Beyond pets, marine life and wildlife face habitat destruction, pollution, and climate change. Students can help by cleaning beaches, supporting wildlife rehabilitation centers, promoting sustainable practices, and educating others about conservation.

Volunteering with animals teaches patience, gentleness, and respect for life in all its forms, especially when caring for injured or abandoned animals. It also fosters a sense of stewardship, reminding us that our wellbeing is deeply connected to the health of the planet and all its inhabitants. Whether you are feeding orphaned kittens, tagging sea turtles for research, or helping restore a natural habitat, your actions make a measurable difference.

Supporting animals in any environment, urban, rural, or wild, is a gift of time and heart that reveals your compassion, sensitivity, and dedication to the wellbeing of others. It also allows young volunteers to develop leadership skills, explore careers in veterinary science, marine biology, or conservation. Every small act ripples outward in the ecosystem of life.

Pets and Shelter Animals

Animal Shelter Support: Help with general operations at animal shelters, including cleaning, feeding, and comforting animals in need.

Clean Cages: Sanitize and refresh animal enclosures to maintain a healthy and hygienic environment for shelter pets.

Foster Animals: Offer a temporary, loving home to animals awaiting adoption, helping them adjust and recover in a nurturing environment.

Organizing Pet Supply Drives: Coordinate donation campaigns to collect food, toys, bedding, and other essentials for animals in shelters or rescues.

Pet Care Clinics: Assist in low-cost or free community clinics offering vaccinations, microchipping, and basic wellness care for pets.

Spay/Neuter Clinic: Support veterinary teams during spay/neuter procedures by preparing supplies, monitoring recovery, or educating pet owners.

Veterinarian Volunteer: Shadow and assist veterinarians or vet techs with basic tasks, gaining insight into animal health and medical care.

Walking Shelter Dogs/Cats: Give shelter animals vital exercise, enrichment, and human interaction through regular walks and playtime.

Farms and Large Animals

4-H or FFA (Future Farmers of America): Club leadership, volunteerism, events, support.

Animal Showcases: Participate in care and showing of large animals like sheep, goats, pigs, or cows.

Farm Animal Care: Feed and support the welfare of cows, goats, pigs, chickens, etc.)

Horse Rescue Organizations: Help clean stalls and rehabilitate abused or neglected horses.

Riding Stable Volunteer: Assist with feed, cleanup, and grooming.

Sanctuaries: Assist at Farm Sanctuary (CA & NY) or Gentle Barn (CA, MO, & TN)

Therapeutic Riding Centers: Assist with grooming, walking, or side-walking horses during children's lessons or adults with disabilities.

Wildlife Conservation

Big Cat or Exotic Animal Rescues: Volunteer at sanctuaries like Big Cat Rescue (FL) or Turpentine Creek Wildlife Refuge (AR) to assist with feeding prep, grounds maintenance, educational outreach, or fundraising for rescued lions, tigers, and other exotic animals.

Elephant Sanctuaries (U.S. & Abroad): Support organizations such as The Elephant Sanctuary in Tennessee or international programs in Thailand, Kenya, or Sri Lanka through administrative work, advocacy, donation drives, or virtual volunteering.

Farm Animal Sanctuaries: Volunteer at places like Farm Sanctuary (NY & CA) or Woodstock Farm Sanctuary to care for rescued cows, pigs, goats, and sheep, while learning about ethical treatment and sustainable agriculture.

Horse and Livestock Rescue Farms: Volunteer at sanctuaries like Gentle Giants Draft Horse Rescue (MD) or Red Bucket Equine Rescue (CA) to groom, feed, and care for large rescued animals.

Marine Mammal Rescue Organizations: Support groups like Marine Mammal Center (CA) or Seal Rescue Ireland by helping with data entry, outreach, beach cleanups, or (for older students) assisting in animal rehab.

National Parks Junior Ranger Programs: Join the Junior Ranger Program or volunteer corps at U.S. National Parks to assist with wildlife education, habitat preservation, and visitor outreach while learning about large mammals in protected areas.

Raptor Rescue and Education Programs: Volunteer with raptor centers such as the World Bird Sanctuary (MO) or Raptor Trust (NJ) to learn about hawks, owls, and eagles, help with feeding prep, and assist in educational events.

Wildlife Rehabilitation Centers: Volunteer with centers such as the California Wildlife Center or WildCare (CA) to help with animal intake, cleaning enclosures, preparing food, and learning wildlife care protocols.

Wolf and Wildlife Conservation Centers: Support organizations like the Wolf Conservation Center (NY) or Mission: Wolf (CO) by maintaining habitats, participating in tours, or engaging in conservation education.

Zoos (Junior Volunteer Programs): Join youth volunteer or docent programs at zoos like the San Diego Zoo, Bronx Zoo, or Smithsonian National Zoo to assist with visitor education, conservation messaging, and exhibit monitoring.

Marine Life and Ocean Conservation

Advocacy Projects: Consider letter writing campaign to legislators and organizations to advocate for environmental protection.

Algalita Marine Research and Education: Join the Youth Summit, cleanup events, or educational programs focused on plastic pollution.

Beach Cleanups: Local organizations, Chambers of Commerce, and civic groups sponsor these or create, organize, and implement your own project.

Billion Oyster Project (NYC): Help restore oyster reefs through school partnerships and volunteer days.

Blue Marine Foundation: Spread awareness of the work of BLUE and conduct research in ocean policy in marine protected areas in UK, Maldives, and the Mediterranean.

Coral Restoration Foundation: Help with hands-on coral nursery work in Florida Keys and volunteer dive programs while helping to restore coral reefs through propagation and outplanting. Great for Scuba-certified students.

EarthEcho International: This organization, founded by Philippe Cousteau, Jr., offers a EarthEcho Water Challenge, youth leadership councils, and virtual STEM events.

Education/Research in Ocean Protection: Research and awareness is necessary to understand where and why these efforts are important now. Look up various organizations that are involved.

Fisheries Assistant: Volunteer in your local fisheries.

Heirs to Our Oceans: Student leaders and environmental advocates can join a youth crew or start one with opportunities to participate in policy advocacy, education, and activism.

Marine Conservation Institute: With the development of the Marine Protection Atlas and the Blue Parks initiative, the MCI supports efforts to conserve marine protected areas, promote ocean policy initiatives, and preserve biodiversity.

Marine Mammal Center (CA): SF Bay Area and Central Coast students can participate in the MMC's youth education programs, public outreach or remote learning opportunities.

Marine Stewardship Council: This organization is focused on seafood certification and supply chain transparency by offering "blue fish" ecolabel on sustainable seafood products.

Mission Blue: Support global awareness campaigns and partnerships to protect marine areas and locations critical to ocean health.

Nature Conservancy, Oceans Program: Take part in the group's community-based ocean conservation programs.

Ocean Clean Up: Projects are available at beaches, plastic recycling, and on the trash vortex in the oceans.

Ocean Conservancy: Join the International Coastal Cleanup, organize local trash cleanups, or volunteer virtually. You can work on independent projects and create a local club.

Oceana: This policy advocacy organization focuses on ocean protection, ending overfishing, and plastic reduction with legal campaigns, sustainable fishing reforms, and celebrity advocacy.

Save the Bay: Opportunities to get involved with San Francisco Bay area restoration work, shoreline cleanups, and youth education programs.

Sea Shepherd Conservation Society: This organization advocates against illegal fishing, whaling, and marine exploitation. Their campaigns use ships and drones to protect marine species.

Surfrider Foundation: Join a local chapter or Surfrider Youth Club (chapters nationwide), help with beach cleanups, plastic reduction campaigns.

World Wildlife Fund, Oceans Division: Partner with WWF in creating sustainable fisheries, marine species protection, coral reef conservation, and marine biodiversity efforts.

Chapter 5:
Children, Education, Sports

Within the worlds of education, tutoring, coaching, and training, you can take numerous pathways. You can write, research, teach, and spread awareness. You cah coach, train, referee, or umpire in athletics or sporting events. As a volunteer, helping your community members, you lift them up to improve the entire city, region, or state.

Sometimes we do not think about how important people are to our communities. I think of this as "human capital", which is the value of humans in much the same way as monetary capital. Every human has worth that can be strengthened and empowered to be worth more and increase in value. They can be disempowered too so that they feel worthless. Out communities have tons of human capital and you can be the catalyst to raise people up.

With a few moments of encouragement, a kind word, or a helpful suggestion, people can feel good about themselves and go on to accomplish their goals. Remember the times when you had an encouraging teacher or coach. How did that make you feel. This same transfer of good feelings and good words to younger people makes all the difference.

The lists below give you a good place to start thinking about how you can make a difference one person at a time.

Athletics & Team Sports Volunteer

Assisting Local Teams:
Throughout the country, teams need support of all types with equipment.

Athletic Coaching:

All sports need volunteer coaches who give of their time and passion to support and empower kids.

AYSO Referee:

Volunteer referees are trained; officials/referees must pass an official course exam. observational match test, and training programs.

Challenger League Buddy:

Partner one-on-one with a child with physical or developmental challenges to assist them during games and practices.

Community Center Fitness Assistant:

Help lead warm-ups, keep time during drills, or supervise young athletes in public recreational leagues.

Girls on the Run Coach or Buddy Runner:

Mentor and run alongside elementary or middle school girls as they train for a 5K, building confidence and fitness.

Referee Flag Football:

This opportunity allows football lovers to serve and learn.

Special Olympics:

Help coach, support, or cheer on athletes with intellectual disabilities during practices or events.

Sports Camps:

Summer camps need volunteer support in every sport from archery to yachting.

Swimming Lessons:

Drowning is the leading cause of accidental death in kids 1-4 and the second leading cause of unintentional injury death in kids 5-14. Teaching swimming is essential and rewarding.

Umpiring Little League:

With 2.5 million kids playing Little League baseball, there is a great need for umpires.

Youth Soccer Camp:

Assist with drills, games, and supervision during summer or after-school soccer camps.

Academic & Educational Projects

Academic Decathlon/It's Academic/Quiz Bowl:

Serve as a volunteer question reader, scorekeeper, or organizer for academic competitions that challenge students across a range of subjects.

AMC 10/12, AIME, ARML, USAMO/USAJMO Test Prep:

Help students prepare for advanced math competitions by organizing study groups, creating practice problems, or sharing strategies.

Book Buddies:

Volunteer as a reading mentor to support early literacy by working one-on-one with younger students to improve fluency and comprehension.

Book Drives:

Organize community book collections to provide reading material for schools, shelters, hospitals, or libraries in underserved areas.

Boys & Girls Clubs – Reach Out and Read Events:

Support literacy-focused programming by reading aloud, distributing books, or helping children select age-appropriate stories.

Creative Writing Workshops:

Lead workshops that encourage children to express themselves through poetry, storytelling, and journaling in community centers or schools.

Harvard–MIT Mathematics Tournament Prep:

Assist middle or high school teams in preparing for prestigious math competitions through problem-solving sessions or mock tests.

Library Reading Events for Kids:

Volunteer at public libraries to read aloud to children, help with crafts, or support themed storytime events.

Literacy Development:

Tutor refugees, immigrants, or younger students in English reading and comprehension to help them thrive in academic settings.

Little Free Library:

Build and maintain community libraries that promote literacy and provide free books.

Math/Science Enrichment:

Organize fun experiments and projects that extend classroom learning in math, biology, chemistry, or physics.

MathCounts Junior High Math Training:

Coach or assist younger students preparing for MathCounts by leading drills, reviewing concepts, or organizing mini competitions.

Mentor:

Build meaningful relationships with younger students by providing academic guidance, encouragement, and life skills support.

Pen Pal Projects:

Exchange letters with younger students or international peers to build literacy, cultural understanding, and human connection.

Robotics Programming:

Mentor elementary or middle school students in basic coding and robotics through clubs, camps, or competition prep sessions.

Science Olympiad (Biology, Chemistry, Physics, etc.):

Assist teams by hosting subject workshops, or judging events in this nationally recognized science competition.

Teacher's Assistant:

Support classroom instruction by helping with grading, organizing materials, setting up experiments, or mentoring younger students.

Tutoring:

Provide academic support to peers or younger students in need of personalized instruction.

Community Education

After School Clubs/Classes:

Lead or assist in after-school enrichment programs that support learning, creativity, or social-emotional growth for elementary or middle school students.

Art Classes in the Summer:

Volunteer to teach or assist with free summer art programs that offer creative expression and skill-building to children and youth.

Boating Safety Lessons:

Support certified instructors in teaching children or families safe boating practices, life jacket use, and waterway awareness.

Crafting, Crochet, Knitting, Macramé, & Needlepoint Classes:

Teach or help facilitate fiber arts classes to promote creativity, mindfulness, and intergenerational skill-sharing.

Creating Educational Kits:

Assemble themed kits with educational games, activities, and lesson materials for use in classrooms, hospitals, shelters, or underserved communities.

Drug Awareness & Treatment:

Assist local health agencies or awareness campaigns by distributing information, creating posters, or supporting youth-focused substance abuse prevention.

Environmental Workshops:

Lead or contribute to community education on topics like sustainability, conservation, and climate action through hands-on activities and presentations.

Jewelry Making Classes:

Volunteer to teach basic jewelry making while promoting creativity, confidence, and even small-scale fundraising for charitable causes.

Music Lessons & Fundraising for Instruments:

Offer free music instruction or organize instrument donation drives to expand access to music education in underserved communities.

Ocean & Pollution Awareness:

Educate peers or the public on the impact of ocean pollution and marine conservation through workshops, school presentations, or beach events.

Online Educational Programs:

Create or support virtual learning opportunities such as tutoring, video lessons, or skill-based webinars for students and adults alike.

Photography of Animals, Waterways, Nature:

Use photography to raise awareness about local wildlife and ecosystems, contributing to educational materials or social media outreach.

Recycling/Crafting Waste Classes:

Lead creative sessions that turn recyclable or discarded materials into art while teaching the importance of environmental responsibility.

STEM Workshops:

Design or assist in delivering hands-on science, technology, engineering, and math workshops that spark curiosity and confidence in young learners.

Computer Science/Technology

Business Intern (Marketing, Computer Integration):

Support local nonprofits or small businesses by helping integrate technology, improve digital outreach, and streamline operations through basic coding, website updates, or analytics.

Computer Refurbishing and Distribution:

Volunteer to clean, repair, and set up donated computers for schools, low-income families, or community centers in need of technology access.

Computer Training for Kids & Adults:

Teach basic computer skills such as typing, internet safety, email use, and word processing to children or seniors unfamiliar with digital tools.

Cybersecurity Awareness Workshops:

Help organize or lead sessions educating peers or community members about online safety, password protection, phishing, and secure browsing.

Data Entry and Digital Archiving:

Assist nonprofit organizations or libraries in digitizing records, entering survey data, or organizing files for online access and preservation.

Digital Literacy Outreach:

Join or create a program that promotes technology literacy by teaching underserved populations how to use tablets, smartphones, or digital health tools.

Hackathon Teacher:

Guide students or beginners in coding basics and project development during community hackathons or innovation events.

IT Help Desk Assistant:

Shadow IT professionals and assist with basic troubleshooting tasks, device setup, or software updates at local schools or nonprofits.

Online Tutoring for STEM and Coding:

Provide virtual academic support in math, coding, or science to younger students or peers struggling with technical subjects.

Robotics Volunteer:

Support youth robotics teams by mentoring students in programming, engineering, or teamwork during builds and competitions.

Social Media and Web Design Support:

Assist small nonprofits or student organizations in improving their digital presence through website design, blogging, or managing social media accounts.

Tech for Seniors Program:

Teach older adults how to use smartphones, video chat, and social media to stay connected with loved ones and manage daily tasks.

Throughout the country, teams need support of all types with equipment.

Chapter 6:
Nursing Homes & Older Adults

Volunteering with older adults, especially in nursing homes, is a deeply transformative experience that fosters intergenerational connection, compassion, and dignity. Many seniors face isolation, limited mobility, or memory challenges that can lead to loneliness or depression. A simple visit, reading a book, playing a game, delivering a meal, or offering a smile can reignite a sense of purpose, joy, and belonging. These interactions go far beyond service; they create bonds that affirm the value of every life, regardless of age or ability.

In nursing homes, volunteers become lifelines of energy and care. Whether organizing activities, helping with technology, or just listening to life stories, young volunteers help residents feel seen and respected. This exchange of time and attention bridges generations, allowing young people to gain wisdom, empathy, and perspective on aging, health, and what it means to live fully.

Globally, as populations age, the need for intergenerational care and support grows. Volunteers play a vital role in reshaping how society treats its elders, not as forgotten members, but as cherished individuals with rich experiences to share. This work changes the lives of older adults and strengthens the moral fabric of communities, reminding us what it means to be human.

Bingo, Card Games, Scrabble: Bring joy and companionship to seniors by organizing or joining in games that stimulate memory, conversation, and connection.

Dog Walking: Assist seniors by walking their pets, ensuring both the animals and their owners experience continued companionship and daily care.

Errands: Support older adults by running errands such as grocery shopping, pharmacy pickups, or mailing packages when mobility or transportation is limited.

Food Delivery: Volunteer to deliver hot meals or groceries to homebound seniors, offering both nutrition and a friendly face.

Hospice Care: Provide compassionate companionship to individuals in end-of-life care through quiet presence, conversation, and emotional support.

Meals on Wheels: Help deliver nutritious meals to seniors through a structured community program that also checks in on their well-being.

Nursing Homes: Volunteer in nursing homes by assisting with activities, offering one-on-one visits, or helping staff create a warm, engaging environment.

Reading Books to Seniors: Offer companionship and mental stimulation by reading aloud to seniors, including those with visual impairments or memory challenges.

Senior Centers: Support community senior centers by helping with events, classes, or social programs that promote engagement and independence.

Technology Training: Teach older adults how to use smartphones, email, video calls, or social media so they can stay connected and confident in a digital world.

Yard Work: Lend a hand with outdoor chores like raking, weeding, or planting to help seniors maintain their homes and enjoy their outdoor spaces.

Chapter 7:
Environment & Outdoors

Beach and Lake Clean-ups:
Remove litter from shorelines to protect marine ecosystems, improve water quality, and preserve natural beauty for wildlife and communities.

Community Litter/Trash Pickup:
Clean up neighborhoods, parks, and roadways to reduce pollution and promote civic pride and environmental responsibility.

Fire Prevention:
Volunteer with forest or fire services to educate the public, clear dry brush, and implement safety measures to reduce wildfire risks.

Forest Renewal:
Support reforestation efforts by planting native trees, restoring habitats, and maintaining trails to encourage biodiversity and environmental balance.

Invasive Species Removal:
Help remove non-native plants or animals that threaten local ecosystems, allowing native species to thrive.

Marine & Fish Habitat Protection:
Participate in projects that restore coastal reefs, riverbanks, or breeding zones vital to aquatic life.

Pollution Abatement:
Assist in community education or cleanup projects aimed at reducing harmful pollutants in air, water, and soil.

Recycling Cans, Bottles, Metal:
Collect and sort recyclables to keep valuable materials out of landfills and reduce environmental strain.

Swamp Land Protection:
Engage in efforts to preserve wetlands and swamp ecosystems, which provide natural flood control and wildlife habitats.

Tree, Shrub, and Flower Planting at Schools/Parks:
Enhance and beautify local green spaces while improving air quality and biodiversity.

Wastewater Treatment:
Volunteer to educate the public or support facilities that manage water recycling and treatment for environmental health.

Wetlands Conservation:

Protect wetland areas by supporting restoration, water testing, or advocacy efforts that preserve crucial habitats and natural filters.

Environmental Organizations

Friends of the Earth:

Advocate for environmental justice and sustainable policies worldwide through activism, research, and grassroots organizing.

Greenpeace:

Join global campaigns focused on climate action, deforestation, ocean protection, and ending environmental destruction through direct action and advocacy.

Nature Conservancy:

Volunteer with a science-driven organization that protects lands and waters through restoration projects, research, and conservation partnerships.

Ocean Conservancy:

Support efforts to reduce marine debris, protect ocean ecosystems, and influence policy to safeguard coastal environments.

Sierra Club:

Engage in environmental activism, conservation campaigns, and community education to promote sustainability and combat climate change.

Surfrider Foundation:

Volunteer in coastal cleanups, ocean-friendly campaigns, and policy advocacy to protect oceans and beaches.

Sustainable Surf:

Promote eco-conscious surfing, reduce plastic pollution, and support climate-resilient coastal communities through action and outreach.

World Wildlife Fund (WWF):

Support global efforts to conserve wildlife, reduce carbon footprints, and promote harmony between people and nature.

Outdoor Volunteer Activities

Campsite Renewal:

Restore public and scout campsites by clearing debris, repairing facilities, and maintaining safe, clean environments for future visitors.

Composting & Gardening:

Support sustainable living by managing compost systems and nurturing gardens that reduce food waste and promote healthy soil.

Gardening – Building/Refurbishing Gardening Beds:

Construct or revitalize raised beds in schools, parks, or communities to create beautiful, functional spaces for growing vegetables and native plants.

Park and Trail Development and Repair:

Improve public spaces by building or repairing trails, bridges, signage, or rest areas to increase accessibility and safety for all users.

Repainting Fences, Benches, and Bus Stops:

Refresh and beautify outdoor structures with a fresh coat of paint, restoring pride and usability in shared public areas.

Sign Posting/Directions:

Install or repair directional and informational signs in parks, trails, or campuses to enhance navigation, safety, and user experience.

Chapter 8:
Medicine & Healthcare

Projects in Medicine & Healthcare

Blanket Making for Hospitals:
Create handmade fleece or quilted blankets to provide warmth, comfort, and encouragement to hospitalized patients, especially children and those in long-term care.

Buddy-Bracelets/Rocks for Hospitals:
Craft friendship bracelets or decorate kindness rocks to deliver uplifting messages to patients in hospitals, offering a small but meaningful gesture of support and cheer.

Candystriper:
Serve as a hospital volunteer (traditionally in a red-and-white striped uniform) by assisting staff, delivering items to patients, or escorting visitors throughout the facility.

Drug & Alcohol Abuse Support:
Support prevention and recovery efforts by volunteering with local health agencies or nonprofits to distribute educational materials, organize awareness campaigns, or assist at outreach events.

Hat and Scarf-Making for Cancer Patients:
Knit or crochet hats and scarves to provide comfort, warmth, and dignity to cancer patients experiencing hair loss from chemotherapy.

Hospital Volunteer:
Assist hospital staff by delivering supplies, visiting with patients, organizing activity carts, and helping with administrative tasks in pediatric, geriatric, or general wards.

Medical Clinic Support:
Volunteer at free or community clinics by helping with check-in, organizing supplies, managing patient flow, or providing interpretation if bilingual..

Ronald McDonald House:
Volunteer to prepare meals, clean rooms, stock pantries, or plan family-friendly activities for those staying near hospitals while their children receive medical treatment.

Suicide Prevention:
Partner with organizations like The Trevor Project or local mental health centers to promote crisis hotlines, lead awareness campaigns, or participate in walk-a-thons to support prevention efforts.

Transporting Patients:

Assist with escorting or transporting patients within hospital or clinic campuses, providing companionship and logistical support while ensuring safety and comfort.

Vaccination Centers:

Help with non-medical tasks such as registration, information distribution, traffic direction, or comfort care at mass vaccination events and public health clinics.

Medical Clubs - School Based

American Red Cross Club:

Support health and humanitarian efforts by organizing blood drives, CPR/first aid trainings, hygiene kit assembly, and disaster preparedness education in your school and community.

Be The Match Club:

Raise awareness about bone marrow donation, register eligible individuals, and host drives to support patients battling blood cancers and other life-threatening diseases.

Best Buddies Health & Wellness Chapter:

Promote inclusion by supporting students with intellectual and developmental disabilities through social events, wellness activities, and peer mentorship focused on mental and emotional health.

Care Package Club:

Create and deliver comfort kits filled with snacks, hygiene items, journals, and handmade cards for patients in hospitals, children's wards, or cancer centers.

First Aid & Emergency Readiness Club:

Train peers in basic first aid, emergency preparedness, and disaster response, often in partnership with EMTs or local fire departments.

Future Healers Club:

Explore health careers through hospital shadowing, medical speaker panels, and hands-on experiences while organizing donation drives or health awareness events.

HOSA – Future Health Professionals:

Join a nationally recognized organization that prepares students for careers in healthcare through competitive events, leadership training, and community service.

Make-A-Wish Foundation Club:

Raise awareness and funds to help grant life-changing wishes for children with critical illnesses, serving as a Junior Chapter or Student Ambassador.

Miracles for Kids Club:

Support families of critically ill children by assembling and delivering essential care packages, organizing fundraising events, and representing the organization through youth leadership roles.

NEGU (Never Ever Give Up) Club:

Spread joy to children battling cancer by packing JoyJars, writing uplifting notes, organizing Joy Drives, and serving as a TeamNEGU Student Ambassador.

Operation Smile – Cleft Palate:

Create a club at your school to support global surgical missions by raising funds, spreading awareness about cleft conditions, and participating in student ambassador or leadership programs.

UNICEF Club:

Support global children's rights by fundraising for clean water, vaccines, and emergency relief, and hosting educational campaigns about international child welfare issues.

 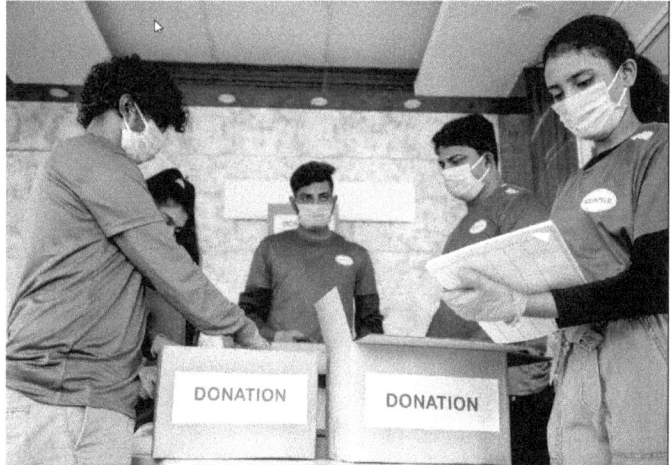

Medical Mission Trips/Volunteerism

Adventist Health International:

Adventist Health International supports under-resourced hospitals and clinics across Africa, South America, and the South Pacific with sustainable health systems and infrastructure. Students can volunteer through affiliated hospitals or support donation drives and missionary outreach coordinated by Seventh-day Adventist institutions.

Africa Cries Out:

Africa Cries Out partners with churches and schools to provide medical aid, food, clothing, and the gospel to vulnerable communities in East Africa. Volunteers may help pack supplies, fundraise, or participate in mission trips offering basic health support and education.

AMEN – Adventist Medical Evangelism Network:

AMEN organizes short-term free clinics in the U.S. and abroad, offering dental, medical, and vision care through a Christian ministry model. Students can assist in patient registration, translation, hospitality, and spiritual outreach alongside professional healthcare teams.

Christian Medical & Dental Associations Global Health Outreach:

GHO sends medical mission teams to more than 25 countries, integrating healthcare with Christian evangelism in underserved communities. High school and college students may serve as support staff, prayer team members, or logistical helpers under mentor supervision.

Club Dust:

Club Dust builds homes, distributes food and clothing, and hosts medical clinics in impoverished communities in Baja California, Mexico. Students can serve on short-term mission teams to assist with construction, sorting donations, or supporting mobile clinic efforts.

Doctors Without Borders (Médecins Sans Frontières):

MSF provides emergency medical care in over 70 countries affected by conflict, epidemics, and natural disasters. While clinical volunteers must be professionals, students can support their mission through fundraising, advocacy campaigns, or internships in communications and logistics.

Faith in Practice:

Faith in Practice provides surgical, medical, and dental care in Guatemala through faith-driven volunteer teams. Students can participate in support roles during mission trips or organize equipment and supply drives through church or school partnerships.

Floating Doctors:

This nonprofit brings healthcare to remote coastal communities in Panama and the Caribbean via boat-based medical teams. Students 16+ can apply to assist with clinic setup, health education, and supply organization on site or through fundraising and pre-trip prep at home.

Global Brigades:

Global Brigades is a student-led nonprofit offering medical, dental, water, and economic brigades in countries like Honduras, Panama, and Ghana. High school students can join university-affiliated clubs or create their own chapter to organize and fundraise for service trips.

International Medical Corps:

This global humanitarian organization delivers emergency medical relief and development services in crisis zones worldwide. While field volunteering is limited to professionals, students can support through virtual internships, advocacy campaigns, and social media outreach.

International Medical Relief:

IMR sends short-term volunteer teams to over 80 countries to provide urgent and preventive care, disaster relief, and community health education. Students age 16+ can assist medical teams with logistics, triage support, community outreach, and patient education.

Loma Linda University Global Health Institute:

This institute coordinates international mission trips and public health initiatives in underserved countries, with a focus on sustainable healthcare and education. High school students affiliated with Adventist schools may engage through pre-health mission tracks, internships, or summer programs.

MAP International:

MAP International distributes essential medicines and health supplies to low-income countries and disaster zones. Students can help raise funds for medical shipments, assist with awareness campaigns, or assemble health kits for distribution abroad.

Medical Missions Outreach:

This organization coordinates surgical and general medical missions across Latin America, Africa, and Asia, integrating Christian ministry and compassionate care. Students can serve on mission teams assisting with patient check-ins, hospitality, children's programs, or evangelism.

Mission of Hope:

Mission of Hope provides healthcare, housing, nutrition, and education services primarily in Haiti and the Dominican Republic. Students can join mission teams to serve in medical outreach, mobile clinics, or community development alongside local healthcare workers.

Missionary Flights International:

MFI supports Christian missions in the Caribbean by transporting cargo, passengers, and relief supplies via aviation. Volunteers and students can assist with packing supplies, ground logistics, or work with partner organizations flying out of Florida.

OneWorld Health:

OneWorld Health builds and operates sustainable medical centers in Uganda, Nicaragua, and Honduras to provide affordable, quality healthcare. Student volunteers can support mission trips, logistics, fundraising, and community health education projects.

Project Compassion:

Project Compassion brings hope and healing to veterans, the elderly, and hospital patients through letter writing, handmade cards, and in-person musical performances or art activities. High school students can volunteer by writing encouragement notes, creating small gifts, or organizing group visits to local VA hospitals, nursing homes, or rehabilitation centers.

Project HOPE:

Project HOPE delivers health education and humanitarian aid around the world, from maternal health to disaster response. Students can contribute through internship programs, assembling hygiene kits, or creating public health campaigns in their communities.

Refugee Health Alliance:

Based in Tijuana, Mexico, RHA offers medical services and mental health support to displaced people and migrants. Students can assist with donation drives, translation (if bilingual), or logistics for medical supply deliveries.

Refugees Around the World:

This initiative supports refugees and asylum seekers by providing food, clothing, medical care, education, and emotional support in regions impacted by war, displacement, or persecution. Students can help by organizing donation drives, raising awareness about global refugee crises, or volunteering with local resettlement agencies and international aid organizations such as the IRC or UNHCR-affiliated partners.

Samaritan's Purse – World Medical Mission:

This Christian organization supports mission hospitals in over 40 countries by sending volunteer medical personnel and supplies. Students can serve at home by packing medical kits, raising funds, or preparing for post-high school field service through its pre-med pathways.

Volunteers Around the World:

Volunteers Around the World is a nonprofit that organizes medical, dental, and public health outreach in countries such as the Dominican Republic, Guatemala, and Vietnam, focusing on underserved communities. While most chapters operate through college campuses, high school students can participate through select pre-health or global health outreach trips, help fundraise for medicine and supplies, or assist remotely with awareness campaigns and logistics.

Blood & Immune Disorders - Research/Volunteer/Fundraising Organizations

amfAR (The Foundation for AIDS Research):

Students can organize awareness campaigns or fundraising events to support HIV/AIDS research and promote stigma reduction in their schools and communities.

Be the Match (National Marrow Donor Program):

High school students aged 16+ (with parental consent) can host donor registration drives, raise awareness about bone marrow donation, and fundraise for patients in need of transplants.

Elizabeth Glaser Pediatric AIDS Foundation:

Supporters can create peer education materials and raise funds for global pediatric HIV care by launching school campaigns or hosting awareness events, such as "Color for a Cause."

GAVI, the Vaccine Alliance – Ebola:

Students can advocate for global vaccine equity through social media campaigns, educational presentations, and fundraising for organizations like GAVI, which distribute life-saving vaccines in low-income countries.

Global Polio Eradication Initiative:

Students can raise awareness about polio prevention through school assemblies, poster contests, or by partnering with Rotary Clubs to support international eradication efforts.

Hemophilia Federation of America:

Volunteer by distributing educational materials, fundraising for bleeding disorder support, or supporting local chapter events during Bleeding Disorders Awareness Month.

Immune Deficiency Foundation:

Support patients with primary immunodeficiency diseases by joining teen ambassador programs, sharing awareness posts, or organizing virtual education sessions.

International Myeloma Foundation:

High school students can raise funds for research, participate in awareness walks, or create educational posters to increase community awareness of blood cancers, such as myeloma.

Leukemia & Lymphoma Society:

Students can join the "Student Visionaries of the Year" campaign, form fundraising teams, and lead outreach efforts to support blood cancer research and patient services.

Multiple Myeloma Research Foundation:

Support this cause by organizing 5K runs, bake sales, or awareness events to fund research and honor those impacted by myeloma.

PEPFAR (U.S. President's Emergency Plan for AIDS Relief):

Students can support PEPFAR's mission by educating peers about global HIV efforts and joining school-based public health advocacy groups that focus on AIDS prevention and treatment.

Sickle Cell Disease Association of America:

High schoolers can participate in Sickle Cell Awareness Month activities, host blood drives, or share social media content that highlights the challenges of sickle cell disease.

Stop TB Partnership:

Raise awareness about tuberculosis through school presentations, letter-writing campaigns to public health officials, or by creating educational videos for youth audiences.

TB Alliance:

Students can advocate for improved TB treatment by sharing fact sheets, launching school health clubs, or participating in World TB Day educational events.

The Global Fund to Fight AIDS, Tuberculosis and Malaria:

Help amplify the Global Fund's mission by organizing student-led fundraisers, developing infographics or posters, and advocating for global health funding.

UNAIDS (Joint United Nations Programme on HIV/AIDS):

Students can create presentations or social media campaigns to share global HIV data, support equity, and advocate for human rights in healthcare.

WHO Global TB Programme:

Support TB prevention and treatment by designing awareness materials, organizing classroom discussions, or volunteering with local health organizations connected to WHO efforts.

Neurological & Developmental Disorders - Research/Volunteer/ Fundraising Organizations

ALS Association (Lou Gehrig's Disease):

Students can participate in Walk to Defeat ALS events, host fundraisers, or create awareness campaigns to support research and care for individuals with ALS.

Alzheimer's Association:

Volunteer by joining the Walk to End Alzheimer's, creating memory care kits for local care facilities, or leading awareness presentations during Alzheimer's and Brain Awareness Month.

Autism Speaks:

Students can become Youth Ambassadors, raise funds through school events, participate in autism walks, or promote inclusion and understanding through peer education.

Cerebral Palsy Foundation:

Support the CPF mission by sharing disability advocacy content, organizing accessible events at school, or raising funds to support research and inclusive technologies.

Epilepsy Foundation:

Students can host purple-themed events during National Epilepsy Awareness Month, promote seizure first aid, and raise funds for research and support services.

IEEE Brain Initiative:

High school students interested in neurotechnology can join student-led STEM clubs to explore brain-computer interfaces, attend webinars, and host brain awareness activities in partnership with local chapters.

National Organization for Rare Disorders (NORD):

Students can raise awareness for rare diseases through school-based awareness campaigns, rare disease day events, or by supporting patient-led storytelling initiatives.

Neurotech Network:

Support the advancement of neurotechnology access by promoting inclusive design, creating informational graphics about assistive tech, or connecting with local rehabilitation centers.

Tourette Association of America:

Students can educate peers about Tourette syndrome, start youth support groups, participate in awareness walks, and advocate for understanding and inclusion in schools.

Organ-Specific - Research/Volunteer/Fundraising Organizations

American Cancer Society:

Students can support Relay For Life events, create care packages for cancer patients, fundraise for research, or lead awareness campaigns on early detection and prevention.

American Diabetes Association:

Volunteer by participating in Step Out Walks, hosting school-wide education events during Diabetes Awareness Month, or distributing healthy living materials in your community.

American Heart Association:

Students can organize Heart Walk teams, host Hands-Only CPR training at school, and lead campaigns promoting heart health and stroke prevention.

American Liver Foundation:

Support liver disease awareness by volunteering at local events, raising funds for research, or educating peers about hepatitis and liver health through school health clubs.

American Lung Association:

Join anti-smoking or clean air campaigns, participate in Lung Force Walks, or raise awareness about asthma and lung health through student-led initiatives.

American Transplant Foundation:

Help promote organ donor awareness through campus campaigns, letter-writing, or digital media efforts, and support patients with transplant-related care needs.

Crohn's & Colitis Foundation:

Support Take Steps walks, start a Gut Health club at your school, or participate in awareness days to advocate for those with inflammatory bowel disease.

Cystic Fibrosis Foundation:

Students can volunteer at Great Strides walks, host school-based fundraising events, or create educational presentations to increase understanding of CF and genetic disorders.

International Xenotransplantation Association:

Raise awareness about emerging organ transplant technologies through research-based presentations, club discussions, and by promoting ethical dialogue around bioengineering.

Lupus Foundation of America:

Participate in the Walk to End Lupus Now, distribute educational materials during Lupus Awareness Month, or host purple-out events to show support.

Muscular Dystrophy Association:

Volunteer at MDA fundraising events like Muscle Walks, support families through letter-writing campaigns, or share facts during Disability Pride Month.

National Kidney Foundation:

Join the Kidney Walk, help with awareness booths about kidney health and organ donation, or coordinate school drives for patient support kits.

National Multiple Sclerosis Society:

Students can form teams for MS Walks, host "Orange Day" awareness events, or lead school discussions on autoimmune and neurological diseases.

Parkinson's Foundation:

Volunteer by organizing Move for Parkinson's events, sharing educational facts during Brain Awareness Week, or supporting caregivers through outreach efforts.

United Network for Organ Sharing (UNOS):

Promote organ donation awareness through student-created campaigns, peer presentations, and National Donate Life Month activities in collaboration with local transplant centers.

Chapter 9:
People with Disabilities

Best Buddies:

Build one-to-one friendships with individuals who have intellectual and developmental disabilities through lunch buddies, peer mentoring, and inclusive school events. High school chapters promote acceptance, leadership, and meaningful social inclusion.

Braille Assistance – Work with the Blind:

Support blind or visually impaired individuals by creating braille labels, transcribing books, or volunteering at vision-support organizations. Some programs also involve reading aloud or assisting with mobility navigation.

Buddy Ball:

Volunteer as a "buddy" in adaptive sports programs where you assist players with physical or developmental disabilities in enjoying baseball, soccer, or basketball. Buddies provide encouragement, safety, and inclusion during games.

Challenger League (Little League Baseball):

Assist children with physical and intellectual challenges during adapted baseball games by helping with batting, running bases, and offering enthusiastic support. Volunteers ensure each player experiences success, fun, and team spirit.

Challenged, Disabled, Handicapped – General Volunteering:

Serve children and adults with disabilities through inclusive community events, tutoring, or recreational activities tailored to individual needs. Volunteers can also support transportation, caregiving, or advocacy projects.

 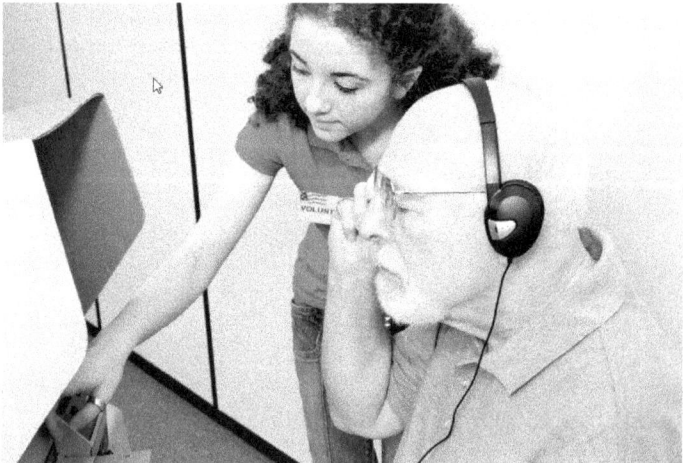

Disabled American Veterans:

Help honor and assist disabled veterans through school-led appreciation campaigns, holiday care packages, or volunteer opportunities at local veteran centers. Students may also help with transportation support or participate in public recognition events.

Easter Seals Youth Volunteer Corps:

Support individuals with disabilities and their families through recreational programs, inclusive camps, and family-centered events. Volunteers can help facilitate art, sports, or sensory-friendly activities.

GiGi's Playhouse Youth Board:

Serve on a youth leadership team to plan events, tutor in math or literacy, or lead fitness sessions that empower individuals with Down syndrome. Volunteers promote acceptance and understanding through education and celebration.

Goodwill Industries:

Volunteer in donation centers, employment training programs, or inclusive retail environments that provide job opportunities for individuals with disabilities. Students can also organize drives or educational workshops on workplace inclusion.

Painted Turtle / SeriousFun Camps:

Support medical camps for children with chronic illnesses or disabilities by helping with pre-camp prep, organizing supply drives, or assisting on-site as junior volunteers. These camps offer adaptive recreation and peer connection.

Peer Buddy Programs / Peer Mentorship Clubs:

Join or start a school-based buddy program that pairs general education students with peers in special education for lunch, class activities, or field trips. These programs foster friendship, empathy, and mutual learning.

Project Linus:

Create handmade fleece, quilted, or crocheted blankets for children who are ill, traumatized, or have disabilities. These comfort items are distributed through hospitals, shelters, and schools.

Sign Language Interpreter – Volunteer Support:

Begin learning American Sign Language and support Deaf or hard-of-hearing students by volunteering at school events or promoting inclusive communication awareness. Advanced students may assist interpreters in supervised educational settings.

Special Olympics:

Volunteer as a coach, unified partner, or event assistant to help athletes with intellectual disabilities compete in sports year-round. High school students can also join youth leadership councils or start Unified Champion Schools.

The Miracle League:

Assist athletes with disabilities during baseball games or adaptive sports events by being a buddy, announcer, or team helper. The Miracle League emphasizes fun, safety, and inclusive community spirit.

United Cerebral Palsy Volunteer Programs:

Participate in awareness campaigns, recreational events, or advocacy efforts to support individuals with cerebral palsy and related disabilities. Students may also help raise funds for assistive technology or family services.

Chapter 10:

Political, Civic, International

Civic/Community Events and Opportunities

Car Wash Fundraisers:

Organize or volunteer at car wash events to raise funds for school clubs, community causes, or nonprofit organizations, while learning teamwork and grassroots fundraising skills.

Civic Engagement:

Participate in voter registration drives, attend city council meetings, or volunteer for local campaigns to learn about governance and influence civic change.

Community Relationship Building:

Host intergenerational events, neighborhood meetups, or cultural potlucks to strengthen bonds among diverse community members and promote inclusive dialogue.

Community Talent Shows:

Volunteer as a performer, host, or behind-the-scenes assistant to help organize school or local talent shows that foster creativity and raise community spirit.

Festivals, Carnivals, & City Showcases:

Support setup, booth management, or activity stations at local events celebrating arts, culture, or seasonal themes while representing your school or youth group.

Fundraisers:

Lead or assist in organizing raffles, bake sales, online donation campaigns, or silent auctions to support local charities, causes, or student initiatives.

Greeting Card Writing:

Create handmade cards with uplifting messages for seniors, hospital patients, veterans, or deployed service members to spread kindness and emotional support.

Musical Events:

Perform at, promote, or assist with benefit concerts, recitals, or open mic nights that raise funds or awareness for local needs or nonprofits.

Parades:

March in, decorate floats, or volunteer with logistics for community parades that celebrate holidays, culture, or civic pride.

Parks & Recreation Support:

Volunteer with local parks departments to assist with trail maintenance, recreational programming, or cleanup days in green public spaces.

Social Media Outreach:

Use your digital skills to promote nonprofit events, campaigns, or awareness weeks by creating content, managing posts, or running youth-led advocacy pages.

Theater Docent:

Greet guests, hand out programs, assist with ushering, or provide educational information about performances at local or school theaters.

Youth Action Corps:

Join a student-led team focused on service projects, community improvement, and youth advocacy, often in partnership with city or nonprofit organizations.

YMCA:

Volunteer at your local YMCA by mentoring younger children, coaching youth sports, assisting with events, or helping in after-school programs.

Charity Walk/Runs

Participating in 5K or 10K charity walks like the Alzheimer's Walk, Heart Walk, Autism Speaks Walk, or Race for the Cure is a powerful act of empathy, unity, and purpose. You will raise money, support groundbreaking research, and promote important issues, allowing you to stand for something bigger than yourself. These walks build resilience, inspire leadership, and prove that every step can bring about real, lasting change.

Alzheimer's Association Walk to End Alzheimer's:

High school students can volunteer by forming a walk team, assisting with event setup and check-in, distributing water, or creating signs to honor individuals affected by Alzheimer's disease.

American Heart Association Heart Walk:

Support heart health awareness by organizing a school team, volunteering at registration or water stations, or creating social media content to promote the event and heart-healthy habits.

Autism Speaks Walk:

Join a youth walk team or volunteer as an event greeter, activity booth helper, or sensory zone assistant to support autism awareness and acceptance.

Juvenile Diabetes Research Foundation – JDRF One Walk:

Students can raise funds, hand out snacks, decorate signs, and help coordinate the walk route to support type 1 diabetes research and patient support.

Light the Night Walk for the Leukemia & Lymphoma Society:

Volunteer to carry lanterns, set up luminaria, assist with logistics, or raise funds to honor those impacted by blood cancers and support cancer research.

Making Strides Against Breast Cancer:

Help organize school fundraising teams, assist with walk-day logistics, distribute pink ribbons, and raise awareness about breast cancer prevention and support.

March for Babies (March of Dimes):

Students can support healthy moms and babies by forming teams, volunteering at family zones or water stations, and helping educate others about premature birth and maternal health.

Out of the Darkness Walks for Suicide Prevention:

Join or lead a school team to walk in honor of mental health awareness, help with registration, or distribute educational materials to reduce stigma and support prevention efforts.

Susan G. Komen Race for the Cure:

Volunteer by handing out water, cheering on walkers, creating tribute signs, or assisting with survivor and family areas while raising awareness for breast cancer research and care.

Walk MS for the National Multiple Sclerosis Society:

Support MS research by joining a walk team, staffing check-in tables, distributing refreshments, or creating motivational posters for participants along the route.

Politics, International Affairs, Military

Advocacy:
Students can raise awareness for causes they care about—such as public health, education equity, or environmental justice—by organizing events, public speaking, or using digital platforms to mobilize peers.

Canvassing:
High school volunteers can go door-to-door, table at events, or make calls to raise awareness, promote voter registration, or support local ballot measures and candidates.

Coalition for Epidemic Preparedness Innovations (CEPI):
Support global vaccine development efforts by organizing school awareness campaigns, fundraising for CEPI-backed initiatives, or presenting on pandemic preparedness and equity in science classes.

CyberPatriot:
Join or form a school CyberPatriot team to compete in cybersecurity defense challenges and promote awareness of cyber safety, infrastructure protection, and tech careers.

Election Support/Poll Workers:

High school students can volunteer during elections by serving as student poll workers, helping with voter check-in, ballot distribution, and site setup under supervision, often through their local county registrar or Board of Elections. They can also support voter engagement efforts by organizing registration drives, phone banking, canvassing, or promoting nonpartisan voting education on social media and at school.

Human Trafficking Advocate:
Students can partner with nonprofits to share awareness materials, host film screenings or info nights, and fundraise for survivor support services in their local or school communities.

Letter Writing Campaigns:
Advocate for legislation, policy change, or public awareness by writing letters to elected officials, corporate leaders, or vulnerable populations, often in coordination with national campaigns or organizations.

NEAP – Naval Engineering Apprenticeship Program:
Apply for this selective summer program to gain hands-on STEM experience working with naval engineers on real-world projects, supporting national defense innovation and technical problem-solving.

Phone Banking:
Volunteer with local campaigns, advocacy groups, or nonprofits to call voters or community members about key issues, events, or policies, helping promote civic participation.

Political Campaigns:
Support political candidates or ballot initiatives by canvassing, managing social media, organizing youth rallies, or assisting with voter outreach during election seasons.

ROTC (Reserve Officers' Training Corps):
Join Junior ROTC in high school to learn leadership, citizenship, and military structure through drills, service projects, and civic involvement.

Social Justice/Social Change:
Lead or join initiatives that address systemic inequalities by organizing educational forums, fundraising for impacted communities, or collaborating with grassroots organizations on youth-led movements.

Town Hall Event Staff:
Volunteer to assist with registration, ushering, note-taking, or microphone handling at local government forums, gaining exposure to civic dialogue and public policy debate.

UNICEF:
Start or join a UNICEF club to fundraise for global child welfare, advocate for youth rights, and promote international solidarity through themed events and campaigns.

U.S. Centers for Disease Control and Prevention (CDC):
While direct volunteering at the CDC is limited, students can participate in teen outreach programs, public health competitions, or school-based campaigns promoting CDC initiatives.

World Health Organization (WHO):
Support WHO's global health goals by presenting research-based projects at Model UN conferences, running health campaigns at school, or promoting international days like World AIDS Day or World Health Day.

Youth Advisory Councils:
Apply to serve on a local or national youth council to advise nonprofits, city governments, or advocacy groups on youth perspectives, policy, and program planning.

Youth & Government:
Participate in YMCA or state-sponsored Youth & Government programs where students simulate legislative processes, debate real issues, and develop leadership skills through mock government sessions.

Refugee Support

Disaster Relief:
Students can volunteer with organizations like the Red Cross to assemble emergency kits, participate in donation drives, or raise funds for communities affected by hurricanes, wildfires, and other disasters.

Food Distribution:
Support local food banks or community pantries by sorting donations, assembling meal boxes, and distributing food directly to families in need at drive-through or walk-up sites.

Housing Services:
Help organizations like Habitat for Humanity or local housing nonprofits by painting, landscaping, assembling hygiene or move-in kits, or supporting fundraising efforts to assist unhoused or low-income individuals.

Immigration Help/Advocacy:
Volunteer with immigrant advocacy groups to prepare care packages, distribute legal resources, participate in awareness campaigns, or support English language and citizenship tutoring.

International Rescue Committee (IRC):
High school students can volunteer with local IRC branches to organize welcome kits, help set up homes for refugee families, or assist with youth mentoring and school readiness activities.

Refugee Health Alliance:
Support this border-based nonprofit by preparing first-aid or hygiene kits, translating materials (if bilingual), or helping with supply drives for displaced families in Tijuana and similar locations.

Translator:
Students fluent in multiple languages can volunteer to translate documents, provide language support during clinics or outreach events, or tutor non-English-speaking students in ESL programs.

Chapter 11:
Religion, Interfaith, Prayer Events
Religious Teaching & Events

Arabic/Hebrew School Teacher:
Assist language teachers in weekend religious schools by helping younger students practice reading, writing, and vocabulary through games and one-on-one support.

Bible, Dharma, Qur'an Classes:
Support religious education by assisting instructors with classroom setup, scripture reading, or helping younger students stay engaged during lessons.

Bulletin, Newsletters, & Livestream Broadcast:
Contribute to your faith community by writing announcements, designing bulletins, or managing livestream broadcasts of services or events.

Candle Lighting Ceremonies:
Help prepare, distribute, or light ceremonial candles during religious observances, while learning the traditions and symbolism behind each practice.

Childcare & Teaching During Services:
Volunteer in nursery or children's programs by supervising activities, leading crafts or songs, and ensuring a safe, welcoming environment during worship.

Christmas Celebrations:
Assist with decorations, holiday meals, pageants, or gift drives to support your church or community center's Christmas outreach and celebrations.

Dwali Celebration:
Volunteer by helping decorate with lights and rangoli, serving food, or supporting temple activities during Diwali festivities.

Easter Egg Rolls & Brunches:
Help organize egg hunts, set up brunches, and create crafts or games for children and families celebrating Easter.

Eid:
Assist with Eid celebrations by helping serve food, greeting attendees, setting up prayer areas, or distributing gifts to children and families.

Event Musician:

Share your musical talents by performing during services, cultural events, or religious holidays on voice, keyboard, guitar, or other instruments.

Holi:

Support Holi events by helping organize color stations, coordinating games and food, and ensuring a joyful and safe environment for all participants.

Outreach:

Participate in outreach programs by distributing food, clothing, or faith-based materials to local shelters, hospitals, or underserved areas.

Peace Events:

Join interfaith or community peace events by helping with planning, setup, and participating in discussions or symbolic rituals.

Plays, Theatre, Religious Showcases:

Act, direct, or assist backstage with religious or cultural plays and showcases that bring faith-based stories and values to life.

Ramadan:

High school students can volunteer during Ramadan by helping organize community iftars (evening meals), preparing food packages for those in need, and setting up prayer spaces at mosques or community centers. They can also create Ramadan awareness projects at school, support younger children in understanding the month's meaning, and participate in service drives that reflect the spirit of charity and reflection.

Social Media:

Manage or support your faith group's social media by promoting upcoming events, sharing spiritual messages, or documenting volunteer service.

Sound/Video Systems During Services:

Learn technical skills by managing microphones, slides, livestreams, and other audiovisual needs during religious services and programs.

Spiritual Sessions:

Help organize or host teen-led or intergenerational spiritual discussions, prayer groups, or meditative sessions at your place of worship.

Sunday School Teacher:

Serve as a youth assistant in Sunday School classes, helping lead songs, crafts, and activities that teach younger children about your faith.

Website Creation:

Utilize your technology skills to design, update, or maintain a simple website for your religious group, featuring calendars, blogs, and service information.

Wedding Event Support:

Volunteer by helping with setup, greeting guests, organizing programs, or assisting with hospitality for weddings held at your house of worship.

Religious Services & Facilities

Beautification of Gardens, Courtyards, Fences, Sacred Spaces:

Volunteer to plant flowers, repaint fences, clean up outdoor areas, or help design sacred spaces to create welcoming and peaceful environments for worshippers.

Church/Synagogue/Temple Band/Choir:

Join the youth or main choir/band by singing or playing an instrument during services, celebrations, or special events to enrich the spiritual experience through music.

Church Volunteer:

Support your religious community by helping with administrative tasks, event coordination, or assisting in weekly programs and outreach efforts.

Greeting Attendees:

Serve as a greeter at religious services by welcoming attendees, handing out programs, and making newcomers feel comfortable and included.

Grounds Maintenance:

Assist with outdoor upkeep by raking leaves, mowing lawns, picking up trash, or helping maintain walkways and parking areas around the religious facility.

Interfaith Councils:
Represent youth voices by participating in interfaith discussions, service projects, or peacebuilding events that promote dialogue and understanding across faiths.

Service/Event Setup & Hospitality:
Help prepare spaces for services or events by arranging chairs, setting up tables, organizing food, and ensuring guests feel welcomed and cared for.

Setting Out Prayer Mats:
Prepare worship areas by neatly arranging prayer mats, ensuring cleanliness, and maintaining respectful spacing and orientation before group prayers.

Setup for Religious Services:
Assist with preparing worship spaces by arranging candles, books, decorations, or materials specific to the tradition and occasion.

Worship & Community Support:
Participate in leading or assisting with youth-led worship, supporting families in need, and helping organize community outreach rooted in your faith values.

Youth Group Leadership/Mentorship:
Take on a leadership role by mentoring younger members, planning faith-based activities, and fostering a positive, inclusive youth group environment.

Chapter 12:
Social Justice & Social Science Research

Houseless & Disadvantaged

Clothing Drives:
Organize or assist in collecting gently used clothing at school or in your neighborhood to donate to those in need.

Distribution to Shelters:
Sort, pack, and assist in delivering donated goods, including clothing, food, and hygiene items, to local homeless shelters or domestic violence centers.

Domestic Violence Centers:
Support shelter residents by preparing welcome kits, organizing donation drives, or volunteering with supervised childcare or community events.

Feed America:
Join local food distribution events, help pack food boxes, or raise funds to support Feeding America's national hunger relief programs.

Food Banks:
Sort, shelve, and pack non-perishable items at regional food banks to ensure families facing food insecurity receive the resources they need.

Grocery Leftover Distribution:
Partner with food rescue organizations to collect and distribute unsold groceries or produce from local stores to shelters and community kitchens.

Habitat for Humanity:
Volunteer for youth-friendly build days, paint and landscape homes, or support fundraising efforts to help provide housing for families in need.

Homeless Shelter Support:
Serve meals, organize donations, or provide companionship through conversation and activity nights at local homeless shelters.

Salvation Army:
Assist with seasonal programs, such as holiday toy and food drives, and back-to-school events, or help in thrift stores and food pantries year-round.

Sock & Blanket Handouts:

Collect new socks and warm blankets, then distribute them with a group in high-need areas or partner with shelters for organized drop-offs.

Soup Kitchens:

Prepare and serve hot meals, greet guests, and assist with cleanup at community kitchens that serve individuals experiencing food insecurity or homelessness.

Toiletry Collection:

Gather travel-sized hygiene products and assemble care kits for donation to shelters, hospitals, or outreach programs supporting vulnerable populations.

Working Wardrobes:

Volunteer to collect, sort, and organize professional attire and accessories to help individuals preparing for job interviews or workforce reentry.

Diversity, Equity, & Inclusion Volunteerism

AFS-USA Volunteer Exchange:

High school students can support international exchange by volunteering with AFS to welcome and mentor foreign students. They may assist with cultural orientation, host events, or promote global understanding through school-based outreach.

AmeriCorps (State & National) – Addressing Poverty:

While full-time AmeriCorps service is for postgraduates, high school students can volunteer with AmeriCorps partner organizations in their local area. Opportunities include assisting with food drives, tutoring, and housing support for underserved communities

Citizens' Climate Education DEI Fellows:

Students can get involved in environmental justice by participating in climate education forums that emphasize diversity and inclusion. They may also support youth-led campaigns that highlight the intersection of climate action and social equity.

Coaching Corps – Coaching Underserved Youth Sports:

High school volunteers can serve as assistant coaches, referees, or event helpers for youth sports programs in low-income communities. Their presence supports physical activity, teamwork, and mentorship for children with limited access to organized sports.

Corporate DEI Volunteer Weeks:

Students can participate in DEI volunteer events hosted by corporations in partnership with nonprofits, focusing on inclusion, equity, and community-building. Volunteer roles may include participating in school supply drives, working in community gardens, or mentoring younger students.

Lutheran Volunteer Corps – Faith-Based National Service:
Although the full program is designed for graduates, high school students can support local Lutheran church outreach projects that align with the Corps' mission. These may include organizing service days, assembling care kits, or helping with neighborhood advocacy.

Points of Light – Connects Volunteers to Social/Civic Causes:
Students can use the Points of Light platform to find volunteer opportunities that align with their interests in education, equity, or environmental causes. They may participate in organized projects or launch service initiatives with school or community partners.

Public Allies – Equity Leadership Training:
Public Allies offers equity-focused leadership development primarily for postgraduates, but high school students can attend public events or collaborate with local partners. They can also shadow leaders or volunteer in youth-serving projects focused on inclusion.

Red Cross DEI Ambassador:
High school students can serve as youth Red Cross volunteers, promoting diversity, equity, and inclusion through events, presentations, and resource sharing. They may lead peer education efforts or help organize inclusive service projects.

VolunteerNow DEI Bridge Initiatives:
Students can join local DEI Bridge programs that foster inclusivity through language translation, cultural celebration, or accessibility support. They may also co-lead community events that build bridges between diverse populations.

Research – Business, Data, Law, International Relations

Excel Input:
Assist researchers by entering, organizing, and cleaning data sets in Excel to support accurate analysis and reporting.

Laboratory Research:
Support scientists by preparing materials, recording observations, and maintaining laboratory equipment.

Literature Reviews:
Help gather, summarize, and synthesize academic sources to support research papers, grant proposals, or scientific inquiries.

National Institute for Environmental Prediction:
Contribute to environmental research or forecasting efforts through data monitoring, analysis, or educational outreach.

Political Science Investigation:

Aid political science faculty, elections, or organizations by collecting polling data, coding interviews, or tracking policy trends for ongoing studies.

Science and Engineering Apprenticeship Program:

Participate in structured summer internships at U.S. Navy research labs, assisting mentors with STEM projects.

Statistical Analysis:

Use software tools or spreadsheets to assist in analyzing research data, generating charts, and drawing conclusions from quantitative studies.

Chapter 13:
Veterans & Military
Veteran Support

Adaptive Sports Assistant:
Volunteer at recreational programs for wounded veterans by helping with equipment setup, cheering participants on, or learning basic coaching techniques. These events encourage physical healing and emotional support through sports.

Flag Placement on Memorial Day or Veterans Day:
Join local efforts to place American flags at the gravesites of veterans during national holidays. This solemn act demonstrates respect and remembrance for those who made the ultimate sacrifice in the service of their country.

Fundraising for Disabled Veterans:
Organize a fundraiser, such as a walkathon or car wash, to benefit organizations that support wounded warriors or adaptive sports programs. These events generate resources for medical equipment, rehabilitation, and long-term care.

Holiday Cards for Heroes (Red Cross):
Join the Red Cross campaign to create and send handmade holiday cards with messages of appreciation to veterans, active-duty troops, and military families. This small gesture brings joy, hope, and a reminder that their service is valued.

Military Care Packages:
Assemble care packages for deployed soldiers that include snacks, hygiene items, games, and handwritten notes. These small comforts from home boost morale and remind troops they are supported.

Military Museum or Memorial Volunteer:
Serve as a docent, greeter, or event assistant at local veterans' memorials or military museums. Students can help educate the public about military history while preserving and honoring the legacy of those who served.

Operation Gratitude Letter Writing:
Write letters of appreciation to deployed troops, veterans, and first responders through Operation Gratitude's national letter-writing campaign. Students can also include these in care packages that are distributed throughout the year.

Support for Military Families:
Volunteer with organizations that provide childcare, meals, or tutoring for the children of deployed service members. Supporting the family helps alleviate the stress placed on military households during deployment.

VA Hospital Volunteer:
Students can volunteer at local Veterans Affairs hospitals by assisting with clerical tasks, escorting patients, delivering comfort items, or helping in recreational therapy. These roles allow students to offer direct support and companionship to veterans receiving medical care.

Veterans Day School Assembly Organizer:
Take the lead on organizing your school's Veterans Day ceremony by inviting speakers, creating tribute videos, and educating classmates about military service. This event raises awareness and honors the veterans in your own community.

Veterans Home Beautification:
Volunteer to paint, garden, clean, or decorate public veterans' housing and long-term care facilities. These projects improve living conditions and provide a peaceful, well-maintained environment for aging or disabled veterans.

Veteran Story Collection (Library of Congress Veterans History Project):
Interview veterans in your community and record their service stories to preserve in national archives. This opportunity fosters intergenerational connection and ensures their memories are honored and remembered.

VFW & American Legion Youth Events:
Connect with your local Veterans of Foreign Wars (VFW) or American Legion chapter to support events like pancake breakfasts, parades, and memorial services. Students often serve meals, set up events, or assist with running raffles and donation tables.

Welcome Home Events:
Help plan or participate in welcome-home ceremonies for returning service members. Students may greet troops, prepare care packages, or help organize celebratory events through local military organizations.

Wreaths Across America:
Participate in the annual wreath-laying ceremony at veterans' cemeteries in December. Students honor fallen soldiers by placing wreaths and learning about the legacy of those who served.

Lizard Publishing, 7700 Irvine Center Drive, Suite 800, Irvine, CA 92618 www.lizard-publishing.com
Lizard Publishing creates, designs, produces, and distributes books and resources to provide academic, admissions, and career information. Our mental process is fueled by three tenets:

- Ignite the hunger to learn and the passion to make a difference
- Illuminate the expanse of knowledge by sharing cutting edge thinking
- Innovate to create a world that makes the transition from dreams to reality

Our books, available on Amazon and other sites include,

Pick some of the books to put here. Medical School Bound, Computer Science, Vet School, Dental School, Psychology, Neuroscience, Data Science, Fashion Merchandising, Architecture, Civil Engineering, Mechanical Engineering, and Aerospace Engineering

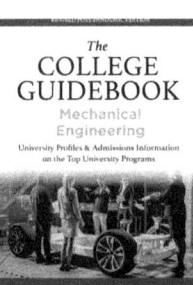
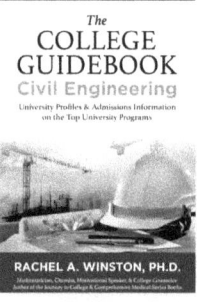

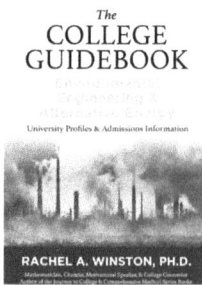

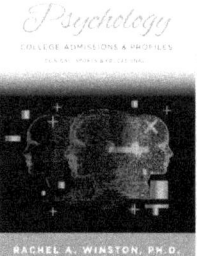

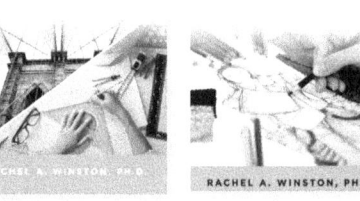

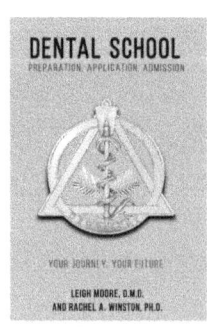
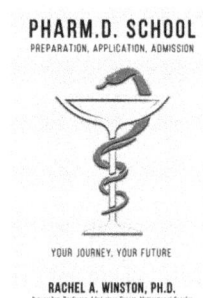

www.ingramcontent.com/pod-product-compliance
Lightning Source LLC
Chambersburg PA
CBHW041153120626
46547CB00020B/3201